Interesting Ways to Teach

Twelve Do-it-yourself Staff Development Exercises

Books from Technical & Educational Services

Obtainable from Customer Services
Plymbridge Distributors Ltd
Estover, Plymouth PL6 7PZ
telephone (01752) 695745 fax (01752) 695699

Preparing to Teach: *An Introduction to Effective Teaching in Higher Education*
53 Interesting Things to Do in Your Lectures
53 Interesting Things to Do in Your Seminars and Tutorials
53 Interesting Ways to Assess Your Students
53 Interesting Ways of Helping Your Students to Study
53 Interesting Communication Exercises for Science Students
53 Interesting Ways to Appraise Your Teaching
53 Interesting Ways to Promote Equal Opportunities in Education
53 Interesting Ways to Teach Mathematics
53 Interesting Ways to Write Open Learning Materials
53 Interesting Activities for Open Learning Courses
53 Problems with Large Classes: *Making the Best of a Bad Job*
253 Ideas for Your Teaching
Interesting Ways To Teach: *12 Do-it-yourself Staff Development Exercises*
Creating a Teaching Profile
Getting the Most from Your Data: *Practical Ideas on how to Analyse*
  Qualitative Data
Writing Study Guides
Improving the Quality of Student Learning
HMA Stationery Ltd *(An open and flexible learning study pack)*

Interesting Ways to Teach

Twelve Do-it-yourself
Staff Development Exercises

Sue Habeshaw
Senior Lecturer & Course Advisor,
Faculty of Humanities,
University of the West of England, Bristol

Trevor Habeshaw
Educational Consultant,
TES Associates, Bristol

Graham Gibbs
Head, Oxford Centre for Staff Development,
Oxford Brookes University

Technical and Educational Services Ltd
REGISTERED OFFICE
37 Ravenswood Road
Bristol BS6 6BW
U.K.

© 1994   Sue Habeshaw, Trevor Habeshaw, Graham Gibbs

ISBN 0 947885 41 2

Printed in Great Britain by The Cromwell Press Ltd. UK

Acknowledgements

We would like to thank all our friends and colleagues who have helped to generate ideas and to test the exercises in this book.

About the series

The series *Interesting Ways to Teach* was initiated with the formation of Technical & Educational Services Ltd in 1984. Since this time the company has continued to produce further books in the series, mostly written by the original authors but increasingly by others. The current list appears at the front of this book.

These books are intended for teachers in further and higher education, though imaginative and flexible teachers and trainers in other sectors have adapted the material to their own situations.

The purpose of the series is to provide teachers with practical ideas for their teaching. While there are sound theoretical justifications for the suggestions which are offered (and often empirical evidence in their support) the emphasis throughout is on practice. The methods which are described in the books have all been tried out, and seen to work, by the authors.

About this book

This book comprises a collection of twelve 'do-it-yourself' exercises based on the books in the *Interesting Ways to Teach* series. The exercises are designed to enable groups of teachers to work together on the ideas presented in the series, to discuss their professional practice and to plan for improvement. The exercises can be used by members of an induction course or staff development course, or simply by the members of any group who are interested in developing their expertise as teachers.

The exercises are based on the principle that, given good materials to work with and clear instructions on how to proceed, groups of colleagues will manage very well without an external facilitator and, in fact, will often achieve more on their own. For clarity's sake, at the risk of being repetitive, the instructions are spelled out in detail for each book in the series.

These exercises have been successfully run many times with groups of university teachers and others. They provide an interesting and sometimes challenging experience for those participating. We hope that you and your colleagues will find them equally useful.

8

Contents   Page

Exercise   Title

Exercise No 1

53 Interesting Things to Do in Your Lectures

Instructions for the organiser: how to run a do-it-yourself activity using *53 Interesting Things to Do in Your Lectures* (Graham Gibbs, Sue Habeshaw & Trevor Habeshaw, 4th edn. 1992)

Timing
The exercise as designed can be completed comfortably by a group or groups of 12 participants in 2 hours. (Smaller groups can spend more time on the rounds or finish earlier. Larger groups can spend less time on the rounds or spend longer on the exercise overall.)

Group size
Minimum number of participants: 8
Ideal number of participants: 12
Maximum number of participants: 15
Large numbers of participants (there is no top limit) should be subdivided into groups of 8 - 15 members.

Accommodation
Ideally there should be a separate working area for each group of 8 - 15 participants, with enough space to set out a circle of chairs in the centre, and tables against the walls.
(If, through shortage of suitable accommodation, you are obliged to run the exercise for several groups in one room, it is advisable to keep the size of the groups small.)

Materials
A copy of *53 Interesting Things to Do in Your Lectures* for each group.
All handouts for participants are provided in the pages which follow.

Before the event

1 Make a copy for each participant of the following materials:
   a Handout for participants
   b Contents page
   and single copies of the following materials:
   c Instructions for the announcer
   d Instructions for the timekeeper
   (If you have more than one group, you will need single copies of **c** and **d** for each group.)
   (Copyright is waived for these handouts.)

2 Get a copy of *53 Interesting Things to Do in Your Lectures* (obtainable from Plymbridge Distributors Customer Services at the contact address at the front of this book).
   Pull it to pieces (physically) so that you have 53 separate items.

Immediately before the event

1 Lay out the 53 items round the room, in order, on tables. An 'L' shape of desks for the items, and a circle of chairs at the side, one for each participant, would do nicely.

2 On a side table set out:
   a Instructions for the announcer
   b Instructions for the timekeeper

At the event

1 Ensure that each participant picks up the *contents page* and reads the *handout for participants* on entering the room.

2 Join the exercise as an *equal* participant.

Alternative ways of running the exercise

1 Instead of allowing participants to choose items, you could allocate them. This would save a certain amount of time and materials and would carry with it the benefits and disadvantages of limited choice. This may be something you decide to do with a group which wants a more focused discussion.

2 In the case of large numbers, you can organise subgroups by subject area if this seems appropriate.

Handout for participants

Glance quickly through these notes.

1   This is a 'do-it-yourself' workshop. All the necessary instructions are provided, although to start the workshop requires a bit of organisation for which your cooperation is required.

2   The person whose name comes *first* alphabetically should take the *Instructions for the announcer.*

3   The person whose name comes *last* alphabetically should take the *Instructions for the timekeeper.*

4   The announcer and timekeeper will need a couple of minutes to glance through their instructions, then the announcer will start the workshop.

5   Everyone, including the announcer and the timekeeper, takes part in the exercise as an equal participant.

6   Enjoy yourself.

Contents

Instructions for the announcer

Glance quickly through these instructions.

1   Get everyone's attention and read out the following message:

I am the announcer and I have to announce things to you. The authors of the book we will be using have sent this message to you:

This session is about making your lectures go better.

We believe that 'experts' are not always useful during such discussions and we are confident that you can have a productive and enjoyable session by yourselves.

There are no other instructions than these I am reading now. If you are confused, don't ask ME; use your common sense.

The first thing to do is to introduce ourselves. We'll do a 'round', starting with the person on my right and moving anticlockwise. We've got a few minutes to complete the round and for each of us to say who we are and what we teach. O.K., let's start with the person on my right.

2   At the end of the round please read the following:

You have copies of the contents list of the book *53 Interesting Things to Do in Your Lectures.* On the tables are spread 53 interesting items. Your task is to look at the list of contents and to select an item you'd like to find out about. Go and find this item and read it. I'll join in too. The timekeeper will tell us when we've had 8 minutes, at which point we will come and sit in the circle of chairs. We are asked...

   a   to explain the item we've read;

   b   to comment on it in the light of our experience of lecturing to students on the courses we teach;

   c   to open up the issue to the rest of the group, asking for their comments, and chairing any discussion which follows.

O.K., you have the list of contents: off we go.

N.B. Remember to participate yourself.

3   After the timekeeper has announced *You have had 8 minutes; please come and sit down* and everyone has sat down, please read the following:

I have an announcement. Just to remind you, when it's your turn, you should
 a explain the item you've just read; then
 b comment on the item in the light of your experience of lecturing to students on the courses you teach; then
 c open up the discussion to the rest of the group. You could ask questions, for example, 'Does anyone else use this method? Could we use it more? What problems can arise as a result of this method? What do other people think?' etc. Then chair the discussion which follows.

The timekeeper will keep track of each 5 minutes of time. We'll go round in a clockwise direction, starting with the person who is nearest the door.

4   When the timekeeper announces *It's time to move on to the last stage of the session*, read out:

I have an announcement. To draw our personal conclusions from this session, the authors suggest that each of us in turn makes a personal statement starting with the words 'One thing I intend to do in my lectures in future is ....'
Please take three minutes to think about your personal statement.

5   After the timekeeper has announced *You have had 3 minutes*, say:

We'll go round anticlockwise, starting with the person sitting nearest the door.

6   At the end of the round of personal statements say:

The authors would like to point out some techniques, all detailed in the book, which were used in this session:
 •   *2 - Flagging: explaining what we were doing to start off with.*
 •   *3 - Ground rules for participants, announcer and timekeeper and the rotating chair for discussion.*
 •   *18 - Article for reading during the 8 minutes.*
 •   *34 - Breaks between the different bits of the session.*
 •   *43 - Quiet time to give an opportunity to collect thoughts.*
 •   *44 - Drama when participants took on roles.*
 •   *45 - Students as teachers during the exercise.*
 •   *46 - Using the audience to provide inputs for the session which were not from the teacher.*
 •   *53 - Are there any questions? in the group discussion.*

Thank you for participating. That is the end of the session.

Instructions for the timekeeper

Glance quickly through these instructions.

It is your job to inform others when the time allocated for a task has elapsed. Otherwise you should participate like everyone else.

1   People have 8 minutes to choose an item and read it before coming back to discuss what they have read. Let them know when 8 minutes have elapsed by saying:

You have had your 8 minutes. Please come and sit down.

2   Individuals have 5 minutes each for their item. When each individual has had 5 minutes say:

We have now spent 5 minutes on this item. It is time to move on to the next item.

   NB   It is very important that you are strict about timing these periods of 5 minutes if everyone in the group is to have a turn.

3   When all members of the group have had their five minutes or when there are 25 minutes left before the end of the session, whichever occurs earlier, say:

It is time to move on to the last stage of the session.

4   When the announcer says, *Please take 3 minutes to think about your personal statement*, time 3 minutes, and then say:

You have had 3 minutes.

Exercise No 2

53 Interesting Things to Do in Your Seminars and Tutorials

Instructions for the organiser: how to run a do-it-yourself activity using *53 Interesting Things to Do in Your Seminars and Tutorials*
(Sue Habeshaw, Trevor Habeshaw, & Graham Gibbs 4th edn. 1992)

Timing
The exercise as designed can be completed comfortably by a group or groups of 12 participants in 2 hours. (Smaller groups can spend more time on the rounds or finish earlier. Larger groups can spend less time on the rounds or spend longer on the exercise overall.)

Group size
Minimum number of participants: 8
Ideal number of participants: 12
Maximum number of participants: 15
Large numbers of participants (there is no top limit) should be subdivided into groups of 8 - 15 members.

Accommodation
Ideally there should be a separate working area for each group of 8 - 15 participants, with enough space to set out a circle of chairs in the centre, and tables against the walls.
(If, through shortage of suitable accommodation, you are obliged to run the exercise for several groups in one room, it is advisable to keep the size of the groups small.)

Materials
A copy of *53 Interesting Things to Do in Your Seminars and Tutorials* for each group.
All handouts for participants are provided in the pages which follow.

53 Interesting Things to Do in Your Seminars and Tutorials

Before the event

1 Make a copy for each participant of the following materials:
   a **Handout for participants**
   b **Contents page**
   and single copies of the following materials:
   c **Instructions for the announcer**
   d **Instructions for the timekeeper**
   (If you have more than one group, you will need single copies of **c** and **d** for each group.)
   (Copyright is waived for these handouts.)

2 Get a copy of **53 Interesting Things to Do in Your Seminars and Tutorials** (obtainable from Plymbridge Distributors Customer Services at the contact address at the front of this book). Pull it to pieces (physically) so that you have 53 separate items.

Immediately before the event

1 Lay out the 53 items round the room, in order, on tables. An 'L' shape of desks for the items, and a circle of chairs at the side, one for each participant, would do nicely.

2 On a side table set out:
   a **Instructions for the announcer**
   b **Instructions for the timekeeper**

At the event

1 Ensure that each participant picks up the **contents page** and reads the **handout for participants** on entering the room.

2 Join the exercise as an *equal* participant.

Alternative ways of running the exercise

1 Instead of allowing participants to choose items, you could allocate them. This would save a certain amount of time and materials and would carry with it the benefits and disadvantages of limited choice. This may be something you decide to do with a group which wants a more focused discussion.

2 In the case of large numbers, you can organise subgroups by subject area if this seems appropriate.

Handout for participants

Glance quickly through these notes.

1   This is a 'do-it-yourself' workshop. All the necessary instructions are provided, although to start the workshop requires a bit of organisation for which your cooperation is required.

2   The person whose name comes *first* alphabetically should take the **Instructions for the announcer.**

3   The person whose name comes *last* alphabetically should take the **Instructions for the timekeeper.**

4   The announcer and timekeeper will need a couple of minutes to glance through their instructions, then the announcer will start the workshop.

5   Everyone, including the announcer and the timekeeper, takes part in the exercise as an equal participant.

6   Enjoy yourself.

Glossary
There is considerable variation in the meanings which different people ascribe to the terms *seminar* and *tutorial*. In this workshop the following definitions will be used:
seminar: a session during which a student (or students) presents a prepared paper to the class.
tutorial: a group discussion, usually chaired by the lecturer.

Contents

Instructions for the announcer

Glance quickly through these instructions.

1   Get everyone's attention and read out the following message:

> I am the announcer and I have to announce things to you. The authors of the book we will
> be using have sent this message to you:
>> *This session is about making your seminars and tutorials go better.*
>> *We believe that 'experts' are not always useful during such discussions and we are*
>> *confident that you can have a productive and enjoyable session by yourselves.*
>
> There are no other instructions than these I am reading now. If you are confused, don't
> ask ME; use your common sense. The first thing to do is to introduce ourselves. We'll do
> a 'round', starting with the person on my right and moving anticlockwise. We've got a few
> minutes to complete the round and for each of us to say who we are and what we teach.
> O.K., let's start with the person on my right.

2   At the end of the round please read the following:

> You have copies of the contents list of the book *53 Interesting Things to Do in Your
> Seminars and Tutorials.* I would also like to draw your attention to the glossary of terms
> on your *Handout for participants.*
> On the tables are spread 53 interesting items. Your task is to look at the list of contents
> and to select an item you'd like to find out about. Go and find this item and read it. I'll
> join in too. The timekeeper will tell us when we've had 8 minutes, at which point we will
> come and sit in the circle of chairs. We are asked...
>> a   to explain the item we've read;
>> b   to comment on it in the light of our experience of running seminars and tutorials;
>> c   to open up the issue to the rest of the group, asking for their comments, and chairing
>> any discussion which follows.
>
> O.K., you have the list of contents: off we go.

N.B.   Remember to participate yourself.

3   After the timekeeper has announced *You have had 8 minutes; please come and sit down* and
everyone has sat down, please read the following:

I have an announcement. Just to remind you, when it's your turn, you should
a explain the item you've just read;
b comment on the item in the light of your experience of running seminars and tutorials.
c open up the discussion to the rest of the group. You could ask questions, for example 'Does anyone else use this method? Could we use it more? What problems can arise as a result of this method? What do other people think?' etc. Then chair the discussion which follows.

The timekeeper will keep track of each 5 minutes of time. We'll go round in a clockwise direction, starting with the person who is nearest the door.

4   When the timekeeper announces *It's time to move on to the last stage of the session*, read out

I have an announcement. To draw our personal conclusions from this session, the authors suggest that each of us in turn makes a personal statement starting with the words 'One thing I intend to do in my seminars and tutorials in future is ....'
Please take three minutes to think about your personal statement.

5   After the timekeeper has announced *You have had 3 minutes*, say:

We'll go round anticlockwise, starting with the person sitting nearest the door.

6   At the end of the round of personal statements say:

The authors would like to point out some techniques, all detailed in the book, which were used in this session:
- **2 - *Learning names:*** *a very brief version to start off with.*
- **30 - *Distribute group roles:*** *for the announcer and the timekeeper and the rotating chair for discussion.*
- **35 - *No-teacher groups***
- **31 - *Working alone:*** *to read items and prepare your presentation.*
- **14 - *Breaking up the task:*** *dividing the material between all participants and dividing reporting into three stages.*
- **22 - *Rounds:*** *to get everyone involved in the discussion, and in making personal statements at the end.*
- **19 - *Furniture:*** *to create a set for display and a circle for discussion.*
- **47 - *Open-book tutorials:*** *since materials were available to everyone during the discussion.*
- **51 - *Self disclosure:*** *in making the personal statements.*

Thank you for participating. That is the end of the session.

Instructions for the timekeeper

Glance quickly through these instructions.

It is your job to inform others when the time allocated for a task has elapsed. Otherwise you should participate like everyone else.

1   People have 8 minutes to choose an item and read it before coming back to discuss what they have read. Let them know when 8 minutes have elapsed by saying:

   You have had your 8 minutes. Please come and sit down.

2   Individuals have 5 minutes each for their item. When each individual has had 5 minutes say:

   We have now spent 5 minutes on this item. It is time to move on to the next item.

   NB   It is very important that you are strict about timing these periods of 5 minutes if everyone in the group is to have a turn.

3   When all members of the group have had their five minutes or when there are 25 minutes left before the end of the session, whichever occurs earlier, say:

   It is time to move on to the last stage of the session.

4   When the announcer says, *Please take 3 minutes to think about your personal statement*, time 3 minutes, and then say:

   You have had 3 minutes.

Exercise No 3

53 Interesting Ways to
Assess Your Students

Instructions for the organiser: how to run a do-it-yourself activity using *53 Interesting Ways to Assess Your Students* (Sue Habeshaw, Graham Gibbs & Trevor Habeshaw, 3rd edn. 1993)

Timing

The exercise as designed can be completed comfortably by a group or groups of 12 participants in 2 hours. (Smaller groups can spend more time on the rounds or finish earlier. Larger groups can spend less time on the rounds or spend longer on the exercise overall.)

Group size

Minimum number of participants: 8
Ideal number of participants: 12
Maximum number of participants: 15

Large numbers of participants (there is no top limit) should be subdivided into groups of 8 - 15 members.

Accommodation

Ideally there should be a separate working area for each group of 8 - 15 participants, with enough space to set out a circle of chairs in the centre, and tables against the walls.
(If, through shortage of suitable accommodation, you are obliged to run the exercise for several groups in one room, it is advisable to keep the size of the groups small.)

Materials

A copy of *53 Interesting Ways to Assess Your Students* for each group.
All handouts for participants are provided in the pages which follow.

Before the event

1   Make a copy for each participant of the following materials:
    a   *Handout for participants*
    b   *Contents page*
    and single copies of the following materials:
    c   *Instructions for the announcer*
    d   *Instructions for the timekeeper*
    (If you have more than one group, you will need single copies of **c** and **d** for each group.)
    (Copyright is waived for these handouts.)

2   Get a copy of *53 Interesting Ways to Assess Your Students* (obtainable from Plymbridge Distributors Customer Services at the contact address at the front of this book).
    Pull it to pieces (physically) so that you have 53 separate items.

Immediately before the event

1   Lay out the 53 items round the room, in order, on tables. An 'L' shape of desks for the items, and a circle of chairs at the side, one for each participant, would do nicely.

2   On a side table set out:
    a   *Instructions for the announcer*
    b   *Instructions for the timekeeper*

At the event

1   Ensure that each participant picks up the *contents page* and reads the *handout for participants* on entering the room.

2   Join the exercise as an *equal* participant.

Alternative ways of running the exercise

1   Instead of allowing participant to choose items, you could allocate them. This would save a certain amount of time and materials and would carry with it the benefits and disadvantages of limited choice. This may be something you decide to do with a group which wants a more focused discussion.

2   In the case of large numbers, you can organise subgroups by subject area if this seems appropriate.

Handout for participants

Glance quickly through these notes.

1   This is a 'do-it-yourself' workshop. All the necessary instructions are provided, although to start the workshop requires a bit of organisation for which your cooperation is required.

2   The person whose name comes *first* alphabetically should take the *Instructions for the announcer*.

3   The person whose name comes *last* alphabetically should take the *Instructions for the timekeeper*.

4   The announcer and timekeeper will need a couple of minutes to glance through their instructions, then the announcer will start the workshop.

5   Everyone, including the announcer and the timekeeper, takes part in the exercise as an equal participant.

6   Enjoy yourself.

Contents

Instructions for the announcer

Glance quickly through these instructions.

1 Get everyone's attention and read out the following message:

I am the announcer and I have to announce things to you. The authors of the book we will be using have sent this message to you:

This session is about assessment. In this session you will be discussing ways of assessing students. Some of these will be things you do already and some will be things you may want to do in the future. The aim of the session is to see if you can develop or improve assessment by, for example, making a more accurate judgement of a student's ability, or making your assessment of students fairer, or less onerous to students, or staff.

We believe that 'experts' are not always useful during such discussions and we are confident that you can have a productive and enjoyable session by yourselves.

There are no other instructions than these I am reading now. If you are confused, don't ask ME; use your common sense.

The first thing to do is to introduce ourselves. We'll do a 'round', starting with the person on my right and moving anticlockwise. We've got a few minutes to complete the round and for each of us to say who we are and what we teach. O.K., let's start with the person on my right.

2 At the end of the round please read the following:

You have copies of the contents list of the book *53 Interesting Ways to Assess Your Students*.

On the tables are spread 53 interesting items. Your task is to look at the list of contents and to select an item you'd like to find out about. Go and find this item and read it. I'll join in too. The timekeeper will tell us when we've had 8 minutes, at which point we will come and sit in the circle of chairs. We are asked...

   a to explain the item we've read;
   b to comment on it in the light of our experience of assessing students on the courses we teach;
   c to open up the issue to the rest of the group, asking for their comments, and chairing any discussion which follows.

O.K., you have the list of contents: off we go.

N.B. Remember to participate yourself.

3   After the timekeeper has announced *You have had 8 minutes; please come and sit down* and everyone has sat down, please read the following:

I have an announcement. Just to remind you, when it's your turn, you should
    a explain the item you've just read; then
    b comment on the item in the light of your experience of assessing students on the courses you teach; then
    c open up the discussion to the rest of the group. You could ask questions, for example, 'How does this method help us to assess our students fairly? Could we use it more? What problems can arise as a result of this method? What do other people think?' etc. Then chair the discussion which follows.

The timekeeper will keep track of each 5 minutes of time. We'll go round in a clockwise direction, starting with the person who is nearest the door.

4   When the timekeeper announces *It's time to move on to the last stage of the session*, read out:

I have an announcement. To draw our personal conclusions from this session, the authors suggest that each of us in turn makes a personal statement starting with the words

'One way in which our assessment system could be better for our students would be .... and one way in which the assessment system could be better for me would be ...'

Please take three minutes to think about your personal statement.

5   After the timekeeper has announced *You have had 3 minutes*, say:

We'll go round anticlockwise, starting with the person sitting nearest the door.

6   At the end of the round of personal statements say:

Thank you for participating. That is the end of the session.

Instructions for the timekeeper

Glance quickly through these instructions.

It is your job to inform others when the time allocated for a task has elapsed. Otherwise you should participate like everyone else.

1   People have 8 minutes to choose an item and read it before coming back to discuss what they have read. Let them know when 8 minutes have elapsed by saying:

You have had your 8 minutes. Please come and sit down.

2   Individuals have 5 minutes each for their item. When each individual has had 5 minutes say:

We have now spent 5 minutes on this item. It is time to move on to the next item.

NB   It is very important that you are strict about timing these periods of 5 minutes if everyone in the group is to have a turn.

3   When all members of the group have had their five minutes or when there are 25 minutes left before the end of the session, whichever occurs earlier, say:

It is time to move on to the last stage of the session.

4   When the announcer says, *Please take 3 minutes to think about your personal statement*, time 3 minutes, and then say:

You have had 3 minutes.

Exercise No 4

53 Interesting Ways of Helping Your Students to Study

Instructions for the organiser: how to run a do-it-yourself activity using *53 Interesting Ways of Helping Your Students to Study*
(Trevor Habeshaw, Sue Habeshaw & Graham Gibbs, 2nd edn. 1989)

Timing
The exercise as designed can be completed comfortably by a group or groups of 12 participants in 2 hours. (Smaller groups can spend more time on the rounds or finish earlier. Larger groups can spend less time on the rounds or spend longer on the exercise overall.)

Group size
Minimum number of participants:	8
Ideal number of participants:	12
Maximum number of participants:	15

Large numbers of participants (there is no top limit) should be subdivided into groups of 8 - 15 members.

Accommodation
Ideally there should be a separate working area for each group of 8 - 15 participants, with enough space to set out a circle of chairs in the centre, and tables against the walls.
(If, through shortage of suitable accommodation, you are obliged to run the exercise for several groups in one room, it is advisable to keep the size of the groups small.)

Materials
A copy of *53 Interesting Ways of Helping Your Students to Study* for each group.
All handouts for participants are provided in the pages which follow.

Before the event

1 Make a copy for each participant of the following materials:
 a Handout for participants
 b Contents page
 and single copies of the following materials:
 c Instructions for the announcer
 d Instructions for the timekeeper
 (If you have more than one group, you will need single copies of **c** and **d** for each group.)
 (Copyright is waived for these handouts.)

2 Get a copy of *53 Interesting Ways of Helping Your Students to Study* (obtainable from Plymbridge Distributors Customer Services at the contact address at the front of this book). Pull it to pieces (physically) so that you have 53 separate items.

Immediately before the event

1 Lay out the 53 items round the room, in order, on tables. An 'L' shape of desks for the items, and a circle of chairs at the side, one for each participant, would do nicely.

2 On a side table set out:
 a Instructions for the announcer
 b Instructions for the timekeeper

At the event

1 Ensure that each participant picks up the *contents page* and reads the *handout for participants* on entering the room.

2 Join the exercise as an *equal* participant.

Alternative ways of running the exercise

1 Instead of allowing participants to choose items, you could allocate them. This would save a certain amount of time and materials and would carry with it the benefits and disadvantages of limited choice. This may be something you decide to do with a group which wants a more focused discussion.

2 In the case of large numbers, you can organise subgroups by subject area if this seems appropriate.

Handout for participants

Glance quickly through these notes.

1   This is a 'do-it-yourself' workshop. All the necessary instructions are provided, although to start the workshop requires a bit of organisation for which your cooperation is required.

2   The person whose name comes *first* alphabetically should take the *Instructions for the announcer.*

3   The person whose name comes *last* alphabetically should take the *Instructions for the timekeeper.*

4   The announcer and timekeeper will need a couple of minutes to glance through their instructions, then the announcer will start the workshop.

5   Everyone, including the announcer and the timekeeper, takes part in the exercise as an equal participant.

6   Enjoy yourself.

Contents

Instructions for the announcer

Glance quickly through these instructions.

1   Get everyone's attention and read out the following message:

I am the announcer and I have to announce things to you. The authors of the book we will be using have sent this message to you:

This session is about study skills. In this session you will be discussing ways of helping your students to study. Some of these will be things you do already and some will be things you may want to do in the future. The aim of the session is to identify some ways of helping your students to study more effectively.

We believe that 'experts' are not always useful during such discussions and we are confident that you can have a productive and enjoyable session by yourselves.

There are no other instructions than these I am reading now. If you are confused, don't ask ME; use your common sense.

The first thing to do is to introduce ourselves. We'll do a 'round', starting with the person on my right and moving anticlockwise. We've got a few minutes to complete the round and for each of us to say who we are and what we teach. O.K., let's start with the person on my right.

2   At the end of the round please read the following:

You have copies of the contents list of the book *53 Interesting Ways of Helping Your Students to Study*.

On the tables are spread 53 interesting items. Your task is to look at the list of contents and to select an item you'd like to find out about. Go and find this item and read it. I'll join in too. The timekeeper will tell us when we've had 8 minutes, at which point we will come and sit in the circle of chairs. We are asked...

a   to explain the item we've read;
b   to comment on it in the light of our experience of helping students to study;
c   to open up the issue to the rest of the group, asking for their comments, and chairing any discussion which follows.

O.K., you have the list of contents: off we go.

N.B. Remember to participate yourself.

3   After the timekeeper has announced *You have had 8 minutes; please come and sit down* and everyone has sat down, please read the following:

I have an announcement. Just to remind you, when it's your turn, you should
  a explain the item you've just read; then
  b comment on the item in the light of your experience of helping students to study; then
  c open up the discussion to the rest of the group. You could ask questions, for example, 'Does this sound like a good way of helping students to study? Could we use it more? What problems can arise as a result of this method? What do other people think?' etc. Then chair the discussion which follows.

The timekeeper will keep track of each 5 minutes of time. We'll go round in a clockwise direction, starting with the person who is nearest the door.

4   When the timekeeper announces *It's time to move on to the last stage of the session*, read out:

I have an announcement. To draw our personal conclusions from this session, the authors suggest that each of us in turn makes a personal statement starting with the words

'One way in which my department could help students to study more effectively would be ...; and
One way in which I'm going to try to help my students to study more effectively is ...'

Please take three minutes to think about your personal statement.

5   After the timekeeper has announced *You have had 3 minutes*, say:

We'll go round anticlockwise, starting with the person sitting nearest the door.

6   At the end of the round of personal statements say:

Thank you for participating. That is the end of the session.

Instructions for the timekeeper

Glance quickly through these instructions.

It is your job to inform others when the time allocated for a task has elapsed. Otherwise you should participate like everyone else.

1   People have 8 minutes to choose an item and read it before coming back to discuss what they have read. Let them know when 8 minutes have elapsed by saying:

You have had your 8 minutes. Please come and sit down.

2   Individuals have 5 minutes each for their item. When each individual has had 5 minutes say:

We have now spent 5 minutes on this item. It is time to move on to the next item.

NB   It is very important that you are strict about timing these periods of 5 minutes if everyone in the group is to have a turn.

3   When all members of the group have had their five minutes or when there are 25 minutes left before the end of the session, whichever occurs earlier, say:

It is time to move on to the last stage of the session.

4   When the announcer says, *Please take 3 minutes to think about your personal statement*, time 3 minutes, and then say:

You have had 3 minutes.

Exercise No 5

53 Interesting Ways to Appraise Your Teaching

Instructions for the organiser: how to run a do-it-yourself activity using *53 Interesting Ways to Appraise Your Teaching* (Graham Gibbs, Sue Habeshaw & Trevor Habeshaw 2nd edn. 1989)

Timing

The exercise as designed can be completed comfortably by a group or groups of 12 participants in 2 hours. (Smaller groups can spend more time on the rounds or finish earlier. Larger groups can spend less time on the rounds or spend longer on the exercise overall.)

Group size

Minimum number of participants:	8
Ideal number of participants:	12
Maximum number of participants:	15

Large numbers of participants (there is no top limit) should be subdivided into groups of 8 - 15 members.

Accommodation

Ideally there should be a separate working area for each group of 8 - 15 participants, with enough space to set out a circle of chairs in the centre, and tables against the walls.
(If, through shortage of suitable accommodation, you are obliged to run the exercise for several groups in one room, it is advisable to keep the size of the groups small.)

Materials

A copy of *53 Interesting Ways to Appraise Your Teaching* for each group.
All handouts for participants are provided in the pages which follow.

Before the event

1   Make a copy for each participant of the following materials:
    a   Handout for participants
    b   Contents page
    and single copies of the following materials:
    c   Instructions for the announcer
    d   Instructions for the timekeeper
    (If you have more than one group, you will need single copies of **c** and **d** for each group.)
    (Copyright is waived for these handouts.)

2   Get a copy of *53 Interesting Ways to Appraise Your Teaching* (obtainable from Plymbridge Distributors Customer Services at the contact address at the front of this book).
    Pull it to pieces (physically) so that you have 53 separate items.

Immediately before the event

1   Lay out the 53 items round the room, in order, on tables. An 'L' shape of desks for the items, and a circle of chairs at the side, one for each participant, would do nicely.

2   On a side table set out:
    a   Instructions for the announcer
    b   Instructions for the timekeeper

At the event

1   Ensure that each participant picks up the ***contents page*** and reads the ***handout for participants*** on entering the room.

2   Join the exercise as an *equal* participant.

Alternative ways of running the exercise

1   Instead of allowing participant to choose items, you could allocate them. This would save a certain amount of time and materials and would carry with it the benefits and disadvantages of limited choice. This may be something you decide to do with a group which wants a more focused discussion.

2   In the case of large numbers, you can organise subgroups by subject area if this seems appropriate.

Handout for participants

Glance quickly through these notes.

1   This is a 'do-it-yourself' workshop. All the necessary instructions are provided, although to start the workshop requires a bit of organisation for which your cooperation is required.

2   The person whose name comes *first* alphabetically should take the ***Instructions for the announcer.***

3   The person whose name comes *last* alphabetically should take the ***Instructions for the timekeeper.***

4   The announcer and timekeeper will need a couple of minutes to glance through their instructions, then the announcer will start the workshop.

5   Everyone, including the announcer and the timekeeper, takes part in the exercise as an equal participant.

6   Enjoy yourself.

Introductory exercise

Complete the following sentences:

Evidence which, if I had it, would show my teaching in a good light, would consist of

....

What I'd really like to know about my teaching is

....

The evidence which I'd want to take with me into an appraisal interview would include

....

Contents

Instructions for the announcer

Glance quickly through these instructions.

1   Get everyone's attention and read out the following message:

I am the announcer and I have to announce things to you. The authors of the book we will be using have sent this message to you:
> *This session is about appraisal. In this session you will be looking at various ways of appraising your teaching and preparing yourself for your appraisal interview.*
> *We believe that 'experts' are not always useful during such discussions and we are confident that you can have a productive and enjoyable session by yourselves.*

There are no other instructions than these I am reading now. If you are confused, don't ask ME; use your common sense.

The first thing to do is to introduce ourselves. We'll do a 'round', starting with the person on my right and moving anticlockwise. We've got a few minutes to complete the round and for each of us to say who we are and what we teach. O.K., let's start with the person on my right.

2   At the end of the round please read the following:

You have copies of the contents list of the book *53 Interesting Ways to Appraise Your Teaching*. On the tables are spread 53 interesting items. Your task is to look at the list of contents and to select an item you'd like to find out about. To help you select an item, take a couple of minutes now to complete the sentences on your *Handout for participants*.

3   After a couple of minutes, say:

Use your answers to help you to select an item. Go and find this item and read it. I'll join in too. The timekeeper will tell us when we've had 8 minutes, at which point we will come and sit in the circle of chairs. We are asked...
   a to explain the item we've read;
   b to comment on it in the light of the three sentences we've just written;
   c to open up the issue to the rest of the group, asking for comments, and chairing any discussion which follows.

O.K., you have the list of contents: off we go.

N.B. Remember to participate yourself.

4   After the timekeeper has announced *You have had 8 minutes; please come and sit down* and everyone has sat down, please read the following:

I have an announcement. Just to remind you, when it's your turn, you should
   a   explain the item you've just read; then
   b   comment on the item in the light of the three sentences you wrote earlier; then
   c   open up the discussion to the rest of the group, asking for their comments, and chairing any discussion that follows.

The timekeeper will keep track of each 5 minutes of time. We'll go round in a clockwise direction, starting with the person who is nearest the door.

5   When the timekeeper announces *It's time to move on to the last stage of the session*, read out:

I have an announcement. To draw our personal conclusions from this session, the authors suggest that each of us in turn makes a personal statement starting with the words

'One way in which I want to go about the appraisal of my teaching is ...'

Please take three minutes to think about your personal statement.

6   After the timekeeper has announced *You have had 3 minutes*, say:

We'll go round anticlockwise, starting with the person sitting nearest the door.

7   At the end of the round of personal statements say:

Thank you for participating. That is the end of the session.

Instructions for the timekeeper

Glance quickly through these instructions.

It is your job to inform others when the time allocated for a task has elapsed. Otherwise you should participate like everyone else.

1   People have 8 minutes to choose an item and read it before coming back to discuss what they have read. Let them know when 8 minutes have elapsed by saying:

You have had your 8 minutes. Please come and sit down.

2   Individuals have 5 minutes each for their item. When each individual has had 5 minutes say:

We have now spent 5 minutes on this item. It is time to move on to the next item.

NB   It is very important that you are strict about timing these periods of 5 minutes if everyone in the group is to have a turn.

3   When all members of the group have had their five minutes or when there are 25 minutes left before the end of the session, whichever occurs earlier, say:

It is time to move on to the last stage of the session.

4   When the announcer says, *Please take 3 minutes to think about your personal statement*, time 3 minutes, and then say:

You have had 3 minutes.

Exercise No 6

53 Interesting Ways to Promote Equal Opportunities in Education

Instructions for the organiser: how to run a do-it-yourself activity using *53 Interesting Ways to Promote Equal Opportunities in Education*
(Vicky Lewis and Sue Habeshaw 1990)

Timing

The exercise as designed can be completed comfortably by a group or groups of 12 participants in 2 hours. (Smaller groups can spend more time on the rounds or finish earlier. Larger groups can spend less time on the rounds or spend longer on the exercise overall.)

Group size

Minimum number of participants:	8
Ideal number of participants:	12
Maximum number of participants:	15

Large numbers of participants (there is no top limit) should be subdivided into groups of 8 - 15 members.

Accommodation

Ideally there should be a separate working area for each group of 8 - 15 participants, with enough space to set out a circle of chairs in the centre, and tables against the walls.

If, through shortage of suitable accommodation, you are obliged to run the exercise for several groups in one room, it is advisable to keep the size of the groups small.)

Materials

A copy of *53 Interesting Ways to Promote Equal Opportunities in Education* for each group. All handouts for participants are provided in the pages which follow.

Before the event

1 Make a copy for each participant of the following materials:
   a *Handout for participants*
   b *Contents page*
   and single copies of the following materials:
   c *Instructions for the announcer*
   d *Instructions for the timekeeper*
   (If you have more than one group, you will need single copies of **c** and **d** for each group.)
   (Copyright is waived for these handouts.)

2 Get a copy of *53 Interesting Ways to Promote Equal Opportunities in Education* (obtainable from Plymbridge Distributors Customer Services at the contact address at the front of this book). Pull it to pieces (physically) so that you have 53 separate items.

Immediately before the event

1 Lay out the 53 items round the room, in order, on tables. An 'L' shape of desks for the items, and a circle of chairs at the side, one for each participant, would do nicely.

2 On a side table set out:
   a *Instructions for the announcer*
   b *Instructions for the timekeeper*

At the event

1 Ensure that each participant picks up the *contents page* and reads the *handout for participants* on entering the room.

2 Join the exercise as an *equal* participant.

Alternative ways of running the exercise

1 Instead of allowing participant to choose items, you could allocate them. This would save a certain amount of time and materials and would carry with it the benefits and disadvantages of limited choice. This may be something you decide to do with a group which wants a more focused discussion.

2 In the case of large numbers, you can organise subgroups by subject area if this seems appropriate

Handout for participants

Glance quickly through these notes.

1   This is a 'do-it-yourself' workshop. All the necessary instructions are provided, although to start the workshop requires a bit of organisation for which your cooperation is required.

2   The person whose name comes *first* alphabetically should take the ***Instructions for the announcer.***

3   The person whose name comes *last* alphabetically should take the ***Instructions for the timekeeper.***

4   The announcer and timekeeper will need a couple of minutes to glance through their instructions, then the announcer will start the workshop.

5   Everyone, including the announcer and the timekeeper, takes part in the exercise as an equal participant.

6   Enjoy yourself.

Contents

Instructions for the announcer

Glance quickly through these instructions.

1   Get everyone's attention and read out the following message:

I am the announcer and I have to announce things to you. The authors of the book we will be using have sent this message to you:

The aim of this workshop is to encourage you to reflect on your equal opportunities practice, discuss issues with one another and plan ways of giving support to your students. The workshop is itself structured to give you all equal opportunity to participate.

We believe that 'experts' are not always useful during such discussions and we are confident that you can have a productive and enjoyable session by yourselves.

There are no other instructions than these I am reading now. If you are confused, don't ask ME; use your common sense.

The first thing to do is to introduce ourselves. We'll do a 'round', starting with the person on my right and moving anticlockwise. We've got a few minutes to complete the round and for each of us to say who we are and what we teach. O.K., let's start with the person on my right.

2   At the end of the round please read the following:

You have copies of the contents list of the book *53 Interesting Ways to Promote Equal Opportunities in Education.*
On the tables are spread 53 interesting items. Your task is to look at the list of contents and to select an item you'd like to find out about. Go and find this item and read it. I'll join in too. The timekeeper will tell us when we've had 8 minutes, at which point we will come and sit in the circle of chairs. We are asked...
   a to describe the item we've chosen;
   b to comment on it in the light of our own experience;
   c to open up the issue to the rest of the group, asking for their comments, and chairing any discussion which follows.

O.K., you have the list of contents: off we go.

N.B. Remember to participate yourself.

3   After the timekeeper has announced *You have had 8 minutes; please come and sit down* and everyone has sat down, please read the following:

I have an announcement. Just to remind you, when it's your turn, you should
   a   describe the item you've just read; then
   b   comment on the item in the light of your own experience; then
   c   open up the discussion to the rest of the group, asking for their comments, and chairing any discussion that follows.

The timekeeper will keep track of each 5 minutes of time. We'll go round in a clockwise direction, starting with the person who is nearest the door.

4   When the timekeeper announces *It's time to move on to the last stage of the session*, read out:

I have an announcement. To draw our personal conclusions from this session, the authors suggest that each of us in turn makes a personal statement starting with the words

'Something I intend to try is ...'

Please take three minutes to think about your personal statement.

5   After the timekeeper has announced *You have had 3 minutes*, say:

We'll go round anticlockwise, starting with the person sitting nearest the door.

6   At the end of the round of personal statements say:

Thank you for participating. That is the end of the session.

Instructions for the timekeeper

Glance quickly through these instructions.

It is your job to inform others when the time allocated for a task has elapsed. Otherwise you should participate like everyone else.

1   People have 8 minutes to choose an item and read it before coming back to discuss what they have read. Let them know when 8 minutes have elapsed by saying:

You have had your 8 minutes. Please come and sit down.

2   Individuals have 5 minutes each for their item. When each individual has had 5 minutes say:

We have now spent 5 minutes on this item. It is time to move on to the next item.

NB   It is very important that you are strict about timing these periods of 5 minutes if everyone in the group is to have a turn.

3   When all members of the group have had their five minutes or when there are 25 minutes left before the end of the session, whichever occurs earlier, say:

It is time to move on to the last stage of the session.

4   When the announcer says, *Please take 3 minutes to think about your personal statement*, time 3 minutes, and then say:

You have had 3 minutes.

Exercise No 7

53 Interesting Ways to Teach Mathematics

Instructions for the organiser: how to run a do-it-yourself activity using *53 Interesting Ways to Teach Mathematics* (Ruth Hubbard 1991)

Timing

The exercise as designed can be completed comfortably by a group or groups of 12 participants in 2 hours. (Smaller groups can spend more time on the rounds or finish earlier. Larger groups can spend less time on the rounds or spend longer on the exercise overall.)

Group size

Minimum number of participants: 8
Ideal number of participants: 12
Maximum number of participants: 15
Large numbers of participants (there is no top limit) should be subdivided into groups of 8 - 15 members.

Accommodation

Ideally there should be a separate working area for each group of 8 - 15 participants, with enough space to set out a circle of chairs in the centre, and tables against the walls.
(If, through shortage of suitable accommodation, you are obliged to run the exercise for several groups in one room, it is advisable to keep the size of the groups small.)

Materials

A copy of *53 Interesting Ways to Teach Mathematics* for each group.
All handouts for participants are provided in the pages which follow.

Before the event

1 Make a copy for each participant of the following materials:
   a *Handout for participants*
   b *Contents page*
   and single copies of the following materials:
   c *Instructions for the announcer*
   d *Instructions for the timekeeper*
   (If you have more than one group, you will need single copies of **c** and **d** for each group.)
   (Copyright is waived for these handouts.)

2 Get a copy of **53 Interesting Ways to Teach Mathematics** (obtainable from Plymbridge Distributors Customer Services at the contact address at the front of this book).
   Pull it to pieces (physically) so that you have 53 separate items.

Immediately before the event

1 Lay out the 53 items round the room, in order, on tables. An 'L' shape of desks for the items, and a circle of chairs at the side, one for each participant, would do nicely.

2 On a side table set out:
   a *Instructions for the announcer*
   b *Instructions for the timekeeper*

At the event

1 Ensure that each participant picks up the *contents page* and reads the *handout for participants* on entering the room.

2 Join the exercise as an *equal* participant.

Handout for participants

Glance quickly through these notes.

1   This is a 'do-it-yourself' workshop. All the necessary instructions are provided, although to start the workshop requires a bit of organisation for which your cooperation is required.

2   The person whose name comes *first* alphabetically should take the ***Instructions for the announcer.***

3   The person whose name comes *last* alphabetically should take the ***Instructions for the timekeeper.***

4   The announcer and timekeeper will need a couple of minutes to glance through their instructions, then the announcer will start the workshop.

5   Everyone, including the announcer and the timekeeper, takes part in the exercise as an equal participant.

6   Enjoy yourself.

Contents

Instructions for the announcer

Glance quickly through these instructions.

1   Get everyone's attention and read out the following message:

> **I am the announcer and I have to announce things to you.**
>
> **This session is for teachers of mathematics. In this session you will be discussing ways of teaching mathematics. Some of these will be things you do already and some will be things you may want to try in the future. The aim of the session is for you to identify some ways of teaching mathematics more effectively.**
>
> **There are no other instructions than these I am reading now. If you are confused, don't ask ME; use your common sense.**
>
> **The first thing to do is to introduce ourselves. We'll do a 'round', starting with the person on my right and moving anticlockwise. We've got a few minutes to complete the round and for each of us to say who we are and what courses we teach on. O.K., let's start with the person on my right.**

2   At the end of the round please read the following:

> **You have copies of the contents list of the book *53 Interesting Ways to Teach Mathematics*. On the tables are spread 53 interesting items. Your task is to look at the list of contents and to select an item you'd like to find out about. Go and find this item and read it. I'll join in too. The timekeeper will tell us when we've had 8 minutes, at which point we will come and sit in the circle of chairs. We are asked...**
> >   **a   to describe the item we've chosen;**
> >   **b   to comment on it in the light of our own experience;**
> >   **c   to open up the issue to the rest of the group, asking for their comments, and chairing any discussion which follows.**
>
> **O.K., you have the list of contents: off we go.**
>
> **N.B.   Remember to participate yourself.**

3   After the timekeeper has announced *You have had 8 minutes; please come and sit down* and everyone has sat down, please read the following:

I have an announcement. Just to remind you, when it's your turn, you should
  a describe the item you've just read; then
  b comment on the item in the light of your own experience; then
  c open up the discussion to the rest of the group, asking for their comments, and chairing any discussion that follows.

The timekeeper will keep track of each 5 minutes of time. We'll go round in a clockwise direction, starting with the person who is nearest the door.

4   When the timekeeper announces *It's time to move on to the last stage of the session*, read out:

I have an announcement. To draw our personal conclusions from this session, we are going to do a final round. Each of us in turn will make a personal statement starting with the words

'Something I intend to try is ...'

Please take three minutes to think about your personal statement.

5   After the timekeeper has announced *You have had 3 minutes*, say:

We'll go round anticlockwise, starting with the person sitting nearest the door.

6   At the end of the round of personal statements say:

Thank you for participating. That is the end of the session.

Instructions for the timekeeper

Glance quickly through these instructions.

It is your job to inform others when the time allocated for a task has elapsed. Otherwise you should participate like everyone else.

1   People have 8 minutes to choose an item and read it before coming back to discuss what they have read. Let them know when 8 minutes have elapsed by saying:

You have had your 8 minutes. Please come and sit down.

2   Individuals have 5 minutes each for their item. When each individual has had 5 minutes say:

We have now spent 5 minutes on this item. It is time to move on to the next item.

NB   It is very important that you are strict about timing these periods of 5 minutes if everyone in the group is to have a turn.

3   When all members of the group have had their five minutes or when there are 25 minutes left before the end of the session, whichever occurs earlier, say:

It is time to move on to the last stage of the session.

4   When the announcer says, *Please take 3 minutes to think about your personal statement*, time 3 minutes, and then say:

You have had 3 minutes.

Exercise No 8

53 Problems with Large Classes:
Making the Best of a Bad Job

Instructions for the organiser: how to run a do-it-yourself activity using *53 Problems with Large Classes: Making the Best of a Bad Job*
(Sue Habeshaw, Graham Gibbs & Trevor Habeshaw 1992)

Timing
The exercise as designed can be completed comfortably by a group or groups of 12 participants in 2 hours. (Smaller groups can spend more time on the rounds or finish earlier. Larger groups can spend less time on the rounds or spend longer on the exercise overall.)

Group size
Minimum number of participants: 8
Ideal number of participants: 12
Maximum number of participants: 15
Large numbers of participants (there is no top limit) should be subdivided into groups of 8 - 15 members.

Accommodation
Ideally there should be a separate working area for each group of 8 - 15 participants, with enough space to set out a circle of chairs in the centre, and tables against the walls.
(If, through shortage of suitable accommodation, you are obliged to run the exercise for several groups in one room, it is advisable to keep the size of the groups small.)

Materials
A copy of *53 Problems with Large Classes: Making the Best of a Bad Job* for each group.
All handouts for participants are provided in the pages which follow.

Before the event

1   Make a copy for each participant of the following materials:
   a   Handout for participants
   b   Contents pages
   and single copies of the following materials:
   c   Instructions for the announcer
   d   Instructions for the timekeeper
   (If you have more than one group, you will need single copies of **c** and **d** for each group.)
   (Copyright is waived for these handouts.)

2   Get a copy of *53 Problems with Large Classes: Making the Best of a Bad Job* (obtainable from Plymbridge Distributors Customer Services at the contact address at the front of this book). Pull it to pieces (physically) so that you have 53 separate items.

Immediately before the event

1   Lay out the 53 items round the room, in order, on tables. An 'L' shape of desks for the items, and a circle of chairs at the side, one for each participant, would do nicely.

2   On a side table set out:
   a   Instructions for the announcer
   b   Instructions for the timekeeper

At the event

1   Ensure that each participant picks up the *contents pages* and reads the *handout for participants* on entering the room.

2   Join the exercise as an *equal* participant.

Alternative ways of running the exercise

1   Instead of allowing participants to choose items, you could allocate them. This would save a certain amount of time and materials and would carry with it the benefits and disadvantages of limited choice. This may be something you decide to do with a group which wants a more focused discussion.

2   In the case of large numbers, you can organise subgroups by subject area if this seems appropriate.

Handout for participants

Glance quickly through these notes.

1   This is a 'do-it-yourself' workshop. All the necessary instructions are provided, although to start the workshop requires a bit of organisation for which your cooperation is required.

2   The person whose name comes *first* alphabetically should take the *Instructions for the announcer.*

3   The person whose name comes *last* alphabetically should take the *Instructions for the timekeeper.*

4   The announcer and timekeeper will need a couple of minutes to glance through their instructions, then the announcer will start the workshop.

5   Everyone, including the announcer and the timekeeper, takes part in the exercise as an equal participant.

6   Enjoy yourself.

Contents

The course

Lectures

Contents *(continued)*

Discussion groups and seminars

Practicals, projects and fieldwork

Assessment

Instructions for the announcer

Glance quickly through these instructions.

1   Get everyone's attention and read out the following message:

I am the announcer and I have to announce things to you.
The authors of the book we will be using have sent this message to you:

> *The aim of this workshop is to encourage you to reflect on the problems for staff and students caused by large classes and to consider some of the possible ways of either solving these problems or finding other ways of responding to them.*

> *We believe that 'experts' are not always useful during such discussions and we are confident that you can have a productive and enjoyable session by yourselves.*

There are no other instructions than these I am reading now. If you are confused, don't ask ME; use your common sense.

The first thing to do is to introduce ourselves. We'll do a 'round', starting with the person on my right and moving anticlockwise. We've got a few minutes to complete the round and for each of us to say who we are and what we teach. O.K., let's start with the person on my right.

2   At the end of the round please read the following:

You have copies of the contents list of the book *53 Problems with Large Classes: Making the Best of a Bad Job*. It is a list of problems. These are problems encountered by staff and students in situations where the student/staff ratio is too high and especially in situations where there has been a rapid increase in student numbers without any related increase in resources.

On the tables are spread 53 items from the book, each one dealing with one of these problems. Your task is to look at the list of contents and to select a problem you'd like to find out about. Go and find this item and read it. I'll join in too. The timekeeper will tell us when we've had 8 minutes, at which point we will come and sit in the circle of chairs. We are asked...

    a **to describe the item we've chosen;**
    b **to comment on it in the light of our own experience;**
    c **to open up the issue to the rest of the group, asking for their comments, and chairing**
       any discussion which follows.

O.K., you have the list of contents: off we go.

N.B. Remember to participate yourself.

3   After the timekeeper has announced *You have had 8 minutes; please come and sit down* and everyone has sat down, please read the following:

I have an announcement. Just to remind you, when it's your turn, you should
    a **describe the item you've just read; then**
    b **comment on the item in the light of your own experience; then**
    c **open up the discussion to the rest of the group, asking for their comments, and**
       chairing any discussion that follows.

The timekeeper will keep track of each 5 minutes of time. We'll go round in a clockwise direction, starting with the person who is nearest the door.

4   When the timekeeper announces *It's time to move on to the last stage of the session*, read out:

I have an announcement. To draw our personal conclusions from this session, the authors suggest that each of us in turn makes a personal statement starting with the words

'Something I intend to try is ...'

Please take three minutes to think about your personal statement.

5   After the timekeeper has announced *You have had 3 minutes*, say:

We'll go round anticlockwise, starting with the person sitting nearest the door.

6   At the end of the round of personal statements say:

Thank you for participating. That is the end of the session.

Instructions for the timekeeper

Glance quickly through these instructions.

It is your job to inform others when the time allocated for a task has elapsed. Otherwise you should participate like everyone else.

1   People have 8 minutes to choose an item and read it before coming back to discuss what they have read. Let them know when 8 minutes have elapsed by saying:

You have had your 8 minutes. Please come and sit down.

2   Individuals have 5 minutes each for their item. When each individual has had 5 minutes say:

We have now spent 5 minutes on this item. It is time to move on to the next item.

NB   It is very important that you are strict about timing these periods of 5 minutes if everyone in the group is to have a turn.

3   When all members of the group have had their five minutes or when there are 25 minutes left before the end of the session, whichever occurs earlier, say:

It is time to move on to the last stage of the session.

4   When the announcer says, *Please take 3 minutes to think about your personal statement*, time 3 minutes, and then say:

You have had 3 minutes.

Exercise No 9

53 Interesting Ways to
Write Open Learning Materials

Instructions for the organiser: how to run a do-it-yourself activity using *53 Interesting Ways to Write Open Learning Materials* (Phil Race 1992)

Timing

The exercise as designed can be completed comfortably by a group or groups of 12 participants in 2 hours. (Smaller groups can spend more time on the rounds or finish earlier. Larger groups can spend less time on the rounds or spend longer on the exercise overall.)

Group size

Minimum number of participants: 8
Ideal number of participants: 12
Maximum number of participants: 15
Large numbers of participants (there is no top limit) should be subdivided into groups of 8 - 15 members.

Accommodation

Ideally there should be a separate working area for each group of 8 - 15 participants, with enough space to set out a circle of chairs in the centre, and tables against the walls.
(If, through shortage of suitable accommodation, you are obliged to run the exercise for several groups in one room, it is advisable to keep the size of the groups small.)

Materials

A copy of *53 Interesting Ways to Write Open Learning Materials* for each group.
All handouts for participants are provided in the pages which follow.

Before the event
1   Make a copy for each participant of the following materials:
    a   Handout for participants
    b   Contents page
    and single copies of the following materials:
    c   Instructions for the announcer
    d   Instructions for the timekeeper
    (If you have more than one group, you will need single copies of **c** and **d** for each group.)
    (Copyright is waived for these handouts.)

2   Get a copy of *53 Interesting Ways to Write Open Learning Materials* (obtainable from Plymbridge Distributors Customer Services at the contact address at the front of this book). Pull it to pieces (physically) so that you have 53 separate items.

Immediately before the event
1   Lay out the 53 items round the room, in order, on tables. An 'L' shape of desks for the items, and a circle of chairs at the side, one for each participant, would do nicely.

2   On a side table set out:
    a   Instructions for the announcer
    b   Instructions for the timekeeper

At the event
1   Ensure that each participant picks up the ***contents page*** and reads the ***handout for participants*** on entering the room.

2   Join the exercise as an *equal* participant.

Alternative ways of running the exercise
1   Instead of allowing participants to choose items, you could allocate them. This would save a certain amount of time and materials and would carry with it the benefits and disadvantages of limited choice. This may be something you decide to do with a group which wants a more focused discussion.

2   In the case of large numbers, you can organise subgroups by subject area if this seems appropriate.

Handout for participants

Glance quickly through these notes.

1   This is a 'do-it-yourself' workshop. All the necessary instructions are provided, although to start the workshop requires a bit of organisation for which your cooperation is required.

2   The person whose name comes *first* alphabetically should take the *Instructions for the announcer*.

3   The person whose name comes *last* alphabetically should take the *Instructions for the timekeeper*.

4   The announcer and timekeeper will need a couple of minutes to glance through their instructions, then the announcer will start the workshop.

5   Everyone, including the announcer and the timekeeper, takes part in the exercise as an equal participant.

6   Enjoy yourself.

Contents

Instructions for the announcer

Glance quickly through these instructions.

1   Get everyone's attention and read out the following message:

I am the announcer and I have to announce things to you.

This workshop is about writing open learning materials. It is intended for people who want to start writing open learning materials and for people who are already writing materials and would like some more information and new ideas.

This is a DIY workshop. There are no other instructions than these I am reading now. If you are confused, don't ask ME; use your common sense.

The first thing to do is to introduce ourselves. We'll do a 'round', starting with the person on my right and moving anticlockwise. We've got a few minutes to complete the round and for each of us to say who we are and what we teach. O.K., let's start with the person on my right.

2   At the end of the round please read the following:

You have copies of the contents list of the book *53 Interesting Ways to Write Open Learning Materials*. Chapter 1 on this list may be of special interest to you if you are a beginner.

On the tables are spread 53 interesting items from the book. Your task is to look at the list of contents and to select an item you'd like to find out about. Go and find this item and read it. I'll join in too. The timekeeper will tell us when we've had 8 minutes, at which point we will come and sit in the circle of chairs. We are asked...
   a   to describe the item we've chosen;
   b   to say how useful we think it looks;
   c   to ask the rest of the group for their comments and chair any discussion which follows.

O.K., you have the list of contents: off we go.

N.B. Remember to participate yourself.

3   After the timekeeper has announced *You have had 8 minutes; please come and sit down* and everyone has sat down, please read the following:

I have an announcement. Just to remind you, when it's your turn, you should
a describe the item you've just read; then
b say how useful you think it looks; then
c ask the rest of the group for their comments, and chair any discussion that follows.

The timekeeper will keep track of each 5 minutes of time. We'll go round in a clockwise direction, starting with the person who is nearest the door.

4   When the timekeeper announces *It's time to move on to the last stage of the session*, read out:

I have an announcement. To draw our personal conclusions from this session, we are going to do a final round. Each of us in turn will make a personal statement starting with the words

'Something I intend to try is ...'

Please take three minutes to think about your personal statement.

5   After the timekeeper has announced *You have had 3 minutes*, say:

We'll go round anticlockwise, starting with the person sitting nearest the door.

6   At the end of the round of personal statements say:

Thank you for participating. That is the end of the session.

Instructions for the timekeeper

Glance quickly through these instructions.

It is your job to inform others when the time allocated for a task has elapsed. Otherwise you should participate like everyone else.

1   People have 8 minutes to choose an item and read it before coming back to discuss what they have read. Let them know when 8 minutes have elapsed by saying:

You have had your 8 minutes. Please come and sit down.

2   Individuals have 5 minutes each for their item. When each individual has had 5 minutes say:

We have now spent 5 minutes on this item. It is time to move on to the next item.

NB   It is very important that you are strict about timing these periods of 5 minutes if everyone in the group is to have a turn.

3   When all members of the group have had their five minutes or when there are 25 minutes left before the end of the session, whichever occurs earlier, say:

It is time to move on to the last stage of the session.

4   When the announcer says, *Please take 3 minutes to think about your personal statement*, time 3 minutes, and then say:

You have had 3 minutes.

Exercise No 10

53 Interesting Activities for Open Learning Courses

Instructions for the organiser: how to run a do-it-yourself activity using *53 Interesting Activities for Open Learning Courses*
(David Kember & David Murphy 1994)

Timing
The exercise as designed can be completed comfortably by a group or groups of 12 participants in 2 hours. (Smaller groups can spend more time on the rounds or finish earlier. Larger groups can spend less time on the rounds or spend longer on the exercise overall.)

Group size
Minimum number of participants: 8
Ideal number of participants: 12
Maximum number of participants: 15
Large numbers of participants (there is no top limit) should be subdivided into groups of 8 - 15 members.

Accommodation
Ideally there should be a separate working area for each group of 8 - 15 participants, with enough space to set out a circle of chairs in the centre, and tables against the walls.
(If, through shortage of suitable accommodation, you are obliged to run the exercise for several groups in one room, it is advisable to keep the size of the groups small.)

Materials
A copy of *53 Interesting Activities for Open Learning Courses* for each group.
All handouts for participants are provided in the pages which follow.

Before the event
1 Make a copy for each participant of the following materials:
   a   *Handout for participants*
   b   *Contents page*
   and single copies of the following materials:
   c   *Instructions for the announcer*
   d   *Instructions for the timekeeper*
   (If you have more than one group, you will need single copies of **c** and **d** for each group.)
   (Copyright is waived for these handouts.)

2 Get a copy of *53 Interesting Activities for Open Learning Courses* (obtainable from Plymbridge Distributors Customer Services at the contact address at the front of this book).
   Pull it to pieces (physically) so that you have 53 separate items.

Immediately before the event
1 Lay out the 53 items round the room, in order, on tables. An 'L' shape of desks for the items, and a circle of chairs at the side, one for each participant, would do nicely.

2 On a side table set out:
   a   *Instructions for the announcer*
   b   *Instructions for the timekeeper*

At the event
1 Ensure that each participant picks up the *contents page* and reads the *handout for participants* on entering the room.

2 Join the exercise as an *equal* participant.

Alternative ways of running the exercise
1 Instead of allowing participants to choose items, you could allocate them. This would save a certain amount of time and materials and would carry with it the benefits and disadvantages of limited choice. This may be something you decide to do with a group which wants a more focused discussion.

2 In the case of large numbers, you can organise subgroups by subject area if this seems appropriate.

Handout for participants

Glance quickly through these notes.

1   This is a 'do-it-yourself' workshop. All the necessary instructions are provided, although to start the workshop requires a bit of organisation for which your cooperation is required.

2   The person whose name comes *first* alphabetically should take the *Instructions for the announcer.*

3   The person whose name comes *last* alphabetically should take the *Instructions for the timekeeper.*

4   The announcer and timekeeper will need a couple of minutes to glance through their instructions, then the announcer will start the workshop.

5   Everyone, including the announcer and the timekeeper, takes part in the exercise as an equal participant.

6   Enjoy yourself.

Contents

Instructions for the announcer

Glance quickly through these instructions.

1   Get everyone's attention and read out the following message:

I am the announcer and I have to announce things to you.

This workshop is based on the book *53 Interesting Activities for Open Learning Courses.* This book is for people who use open learning materials, either their own or other people's, in their teaching and want to improve the quality of their students' learning by setting them more interesting and more varied open learning activities.

This is a DIY workshop. There are no other instructions than these I am reading now. If you are confused, don't ask ME; use your common sense.

The first thing to do is to introduce ourselves. We'll do a 'round', starting with the person on my right and moving anticlockwise. We've got a few minutes to complete the round and for each of us to say who we are and what we teach. O.K., let's start with the person on my right.

2   At the end of the round please read the following:

You have copies of the contents list of the book *53 Interesting Activities for Open Learning Courses.* You will see that it is organised in two sections, "Activities in self-instructional packages" and "Activities in group meetings", and eight chapters. You can use the section headings and chapter headings to help you decide where you want to focus your attention.

On the tables are spread 53 interesting items from the book. Your task is to look at the list of contents and to select an item you'd like to find out about. Go and find this item and read it. I'll join in too. The timekeeper will tell us when we've had 8 minutes, at which point we will come and sit in the circle of chairs. We are asked...
   a to describe the item we've chosen;
   b to say how useful we think it looks;
   c to ask the rest of the group for their comments and chair any discussion which follows.

O.K., you have the list of contents: off we go.

N.B. Remember to participate yourself.

3   After the timekeeper has announced *You have had 8 minutes; please come and sit down* and everyone has sat down, please read the following:

I have an announcement. Just to remind you, when it's your turn, you should
   a describe the item you've just read; then
   b say how useful you think it looks; then
   c ask the rest of the group for their comments, and chair any discussion that follows.

The timekeeper will keep track of each 5 minutes of time. We'll go round in a clockwise direction, starting with the person who is nearest the door.

4   When the timekeeper announces *It's time to move on to the last stage of the session,* read out:

I have an announcement. To draw our personal conclusions from this session, we are going to do a final round. Each of us in turn will make a personal statement starting with the words

'Something I intend to try is ...'

Please take three minutes to think about your personal statement.

5   After the timekeeper has announced *You have had 3 minutes,* say:

We'll go round anticlockwise, starting with the person sitting nearest the door.

6   At the end of the round of personal statements say:

Thank you for participating. That is the end of the session.

Instructions for the timekeeper

Glance quickly through these instructions.

It is your job to inform others when the time allocated for a task has elapsed. Otherwise you should participate like everyone else.

1   People have 8 minutes to choose an item and read it before coming back to discuss what they have read. Let them know when 8 minutes have elapsed by saying:

You have had your 8 minutes. Please come and sit down.

2   Individuals have 5 minutes each for their item. When each individual has had 5 minutes say:

We have now spent 5 minutes on this item. It is time to move on to the next item.

NB   It is very important that you are strict about timing these periods of 5 minutes if everyone in the group is to have a turn.

3   When all members of the group have had their five minutes or when there are 25 minutes left before the end of the session, whichever occurs earlier, say:

It is time to move on to the last stage of the session.

4   When the announcer says, *Please take 3 minutes to think about your personal statement*, time 3 minutes, and then say:

You have had 3 minutes.

Exercise No 11

53 Interesting Communication Exercises for Science Students

Instructions for the organiser: how to run a do-it-yourself activity using *53 Interesting Communication Exercises for Science Students*
(Sue Habeshaw & Di Steeds 2nd edition 1993)

Timing
The exercise as designed can be completed comfortably in a session of 1.5 hours.

Group size
Minimum number of participants: 10
Ideal number of participants: 15
Maximum number of participants: 20
Large numbers of participants (there is no top limit) should be subdivided into groups of 10 - 20 members.

Accommodation
Ideally there should be a separate working area for each group of 10 - 20 participants, with chairs set out in a circle and enough space for participants to move their chairs and reorganise themselves into subgroups.
(If, through shortage of suitable accommodation, you are obliged to run the exercise for several groups in one room, it is advisable to keep the size of the groups small.)

Materials
A copy of *53 Interesting Communication Exercises for Science Students* for each group.
All handouts for participants are provided in the pages which follow.

Before the event

1   Make a copy for each participant of the following materials:

   a   **Handout for participants**

   b   **Exercise 1**

   c   **Exercise 2**

   d   **Exercise 3**

   e   **Answer to Exercise 1**

   f   **Answer to Exercise 3**

(There is no answer to exercise 2. Keep copies of the answers to Exercise 1 and Exercise 3 in separate large envelopes until the last stage of the exercise.)

2   Make single copies of the following materials:

   g   **Instructions for the announcer**

   h   **Instructions for the timekeeper**

(If you have more than one group, you will need single copies of **g** and **h** for each group.)

(Copyright is waived for this purpose.)

Immediately before the event

1   Set out a circle of chairs, one for each participant.

2   On a side table set out:

   a   **Instructions for the announcer**

   b   **Instructions for the timekeeper**

   c   **Copies of the three exercises (but not the answers)**

At the event

1   Ensure that each participant reads the **handout for participants** on entering the room.

2   When the announcer is selected, give him or her the envelopes containing copies of the answers to Exercise 1 and Exercise 3.

3   Join the exercise as an *equal* participant.

Handout for participants

Glance quickly through these notes.

1   This is a 'do-it-yourself' workshop. All the necessary instructions are provided, although to start the workshop requires a bit of organisation for which your cooperation is required.

2   The person whose name comes *first* alphabetically should take the ***Instructions for the announcer***.

3   The person whose name comes *last* alphabetically should take the ***Instructions for the timekeeper***.

4   The announcer and timekeeper will need a couple of minutes to glance through their instructions, then the announcer will start the workshop.

5   Everyone, including the announcer and the timekeeper, takes part in the exercise as an equal participant.

6   Enjoy yourself.

Instructions for the announcer

Glance quickly through these instructions.

1   Get everyone's attention and read out the following message:

I am the announcer and I have to announce things to you.

This workshop is for people who are interested in improving the communication skills of science students. (You may be communication teachers or you may be science teachers: it's O.K.)

This is a DIY workshop. There are no other instructions than these I am reading now. If you are confused, don't ask ME; use your common sense.

The first thing to do is to introduce ourselves. We'll do a 'round', starting with the person on my right and moving anticlockwise. We've got a few minutes to complete the round and for each of us to say who we are and what courses we teach on. O.K., let's start with the person on my right.

2   At the end of the round please read the following:

In this session we shall be trying out some communication exercises for science students. They are from the book, *53 Interesting Communication Exercises for Science Students*. We have three exercises to choose from:
Exercise 1, 'What happened to the gelatin plugs', is designed to help students to write up their practicals.
Exercise 2, 'Flow charts', is an exercise in data presentation.
Exercise 3, 'The detergent treatment', gives students practice in arranging data in tables.

Copies of the three exercises are on the side table. In a minute we will have the opportunity to go and choose one.

When we have made our selection, we will sit in groups according to the exercise we have chosen, so that we can confer if we want to. The group doing Exercise 1 will sit over there, the group doing Exercise 2 will sit over there, and the group doing Exercise 3 will sit here. [INDICATE AREAS OF THE ROOM.]

O.K., we've got 5 minutes to choose an exercise. The timekeeper will remind us of the time. Let's go.

N.B. Remember to participate yourself.

3   When the timekeeper says that the time is up, make the following (repeat) announcement:

The group doing Exercise 1 will sit over there, the group doing Exercise 2 will sit over there and the group doing Exercise 3 here. [Indicate areas of the room and if large numbers opt for any of the exercises, encourage them to subdivide into groups of 3 - 5 members.]

4   When people are sitting in their groups, make the following announcement:

We now have half an hour to try out the exercise we have chosen. The timekeeper will remind us of the time.

5   When the timekeeper says that the half hour allowed for the exercises has elapsed, hand out the answers to Exercises 1 and 3 to members of groups 1 and 3. (No answer is provided for Exercise 2.) Then read out the following announcement:

You now have 10 minutes in your groups to talk about the experience of doing the exercise. The timekeeper will remind us of the time.

6   When the timekeeper says that the ten minutes allowed for discussion in groups have elapsed, read out the following announcement:

The rest of the time is available for a plenary discussion. The timekeeper will remind us when the session ends.

7   At the end of the session the timekeeper will give you your cue to make this final announcement:

There are enough copies of all the exercises and answers for everyone to have a full set. Help yourself on the way out if you would like to have copies.

Thank you for participating. That is the end of the session.

Instructions for the timekeeper

Glance quickly through these instructions.

It is your job to inform others when the time allocated for a task has elapsed. Otherwise you should participate like everyone else.

1 Allow people 5 minutes to choose their exercise. If they haven't chosen after 5 minutes, you may need to chivvy them a bit.

2 People have half an hour to do their exercise. Let them know when half an hour has elapsed by saying:

You've had your half hour.

(If any individuals finish in less than half an hour, you can suggest that they try a second exercise.)

3 People have ten minutes to talk in their groups about the exercise. Let them know when ten minutes have elapsed by saying:

You've had your ten minutes.

4 Two minutes before the end of the session, say:

It is nearly the end of the session, but the announcer has one final announcement.

Exercise 1
What happened to the gelatin plugs

This is a practical write-up which has got quite a few things wrong with it. For instance, you can see straight away that it's written all in one block without any subheadings. Your job is to correct the mistakes and produce a well written report. All the factual information you need is included in this version. Remember to pay attention to details like units as well as language and presentation.

Wednesday

What happened to the gelatin plugs
When we came into the lab we found some absolute alcohol and some saturated mercuric chloride and some glacial acetic acid and some formaldehyde (10%) and some potassium dichromate (one and a half per cent) and, last but not least, some saturated aqueous picric acid (these are called primary fixatives) and we poured these onto gelatin cork bores which we had first taken from 10% gelatin solidified in Petrie dishes and measured and put into test tubes but we only filled the test tubes half full. (Petri dishes are named after the man who discovered them. He died in 1921.) Then we left it to see what would happen. When we came back on Friday we noticed that the plugs, which were 8m across and 2m thick before, had changed and the plug in the absolute alcohol was entire and white and hardened and measured 5 x 2 and the one in the saturated mercuric chloride was ditto and ditto and 7 x 2 and the one in the glacial acetic acid was almost dissolved and clear and hadn't hardened and was 2 x 1/2 and the one in the formaldehyde was entire and clear and hardened and 12 x 4 and the one in the p.d. was entire and sticking to the bottom of the tube and orange and hardened and 6 x 1 and the one in the SAPA was ditto but yellow with little or no hardening and 2 x 0.5. All the primary fixatives did different things to the gelatin plugs. Our lecturer said the ones that were bigger or smaller or hardened were the most important ones. The ones that made them harder were absolute alcohol, s.m.c., formaldyhide and potassium dichromate. This is a good thing because this is what fixatives are supposed to be for, isn't it? Absolute alcohol, patassium dichromate and saturated picric acid made the plug shrink a lot; saturated mercuric chloride made it shrink a bit; formaldehyde made it swell. 10% formaldehyde is obviously the best fixative of all. (I'm not sure about glacial acetic acid.)

p.s. I used John and Sarah's results because mine didn't come out right.

Exercise 2
Flow charts

Either...
Draw a flow chart to illustrate a process you are familiar with, e.g. a scientific process you have learned about at college or a technical process you have been involved in at work,

or
Draw a flow chart to illustrate your life so far. Indicate stages in the process and alternatives to the choices which you have made (or which have been made for you) in your life.

Show clearly where your flow chart begins and ends.

Vary the shape of your boxes and the thickness of your arrows according to the message you want to convey.

Exercise 3
The detergent treatment

The following results are based on those published by Weiss and Wingfield (1). Experiments were carried out to investigate the effect of detergents on two oxidation/reduction reactions. (These reactions take place in living cells and are carried out by enzyme systems which are frequently bound to fatty tissue in the cell membranes. Detergents will release the enzymes from the membranes and are used in investigating the mechanism of their catalytic activity.)

The reactions under investigation may be represented by the following equations:

$$XH_2 + Q = X + QH_2 \qquad \text{(reaction E1)}$$
$$QH_2 + Y = Q + YH_2 \qquad \text{(reaction E2)}$$

Q stands for a quinone derivative (ubiquinone) and two types of ubiquinone were used in the reactions: Q-2 and Q-10.

The effects of nine different detergents were investigated, identified mostly by their trade names: Triton X-100, Triton X-165, octyl glucoside, Emulphogen, Brij 35, Brij 56, Brij 58, Tween 20, Tween 80.

Five different assay systems were used to measure the reaction velocities: A, B, C, D, E.

The reaction velocities were recorded in arbitrary units (U) for comparison between the various systems.

Results

Using assay A with Q-10
for reaction E1

Detergent	Velocity of E1
Triton X-100	2000 U
Octyl glucoside	2200 U

Using assay B with Q-10
for reaction E1

Detergent	Velocity of E1
Triton X-100	400 U

Assay C was only used for reaction E2 with Q-10 and Triton X-100 as the detergent. The result was 1300 U.

Using assay D with Q-10
for reaction E2

Detergent	Velocity of E2
Triton X-100	500 U

Using assay E with Q-10
for reaction E2

Detergent	Velocity of E2
Triton X-100	400 U

Using assay A with Q-2 for reaction E1 (U)		*Using assay B with Q-2 for reaction E1 (kU)*	
Detergent	**Velocity of E1**	**Detergent**	**Velocity of E1**
Triton X-100	2300	Emulphogen	.03
Triton X-165	2200	Tween 20	1
Emulphogen	2100	Tween 80	1
Brij 35	2100	Triton X-165	1.3
Brij 56	2300	Triton X-100	0.6
Brij 58	2100	Brij 56	0.7
Tween 20	2400	Brij 58	1
Tween 80	2300	Brij 35	2

Assays D and E gave identical results for reaction E2 when Q-2 was the ubiquinone used with the following detergents:

Detergent	**Velocity of E2**
Triton X-165	1100 U
Emulphogen	200 U
Brij 58	600 U
Tween 80	800 U

For the remaining detergents assays D and E gave the following results with Q-2 and reaction E2
Assay D
Triton X-100 = 800 U; Brij 35 = 1100 U; Brij 56 = 300 U; Tween 20 = 900 U
Assay E
Triton X-100 = 700 U; Brij 35 = 1000 U; Brij 56 = 400 U; Tween 20 = 1000 U

Collect all these results together into a single table, taking care to see that column headings are unambiguous and that no information is duplicated or omitted. When planning your layout, consider what shape you wish your final table to be.

Reference
1   H. Weiss and P. Wingfield, *European Journal of Biochemistry*, 99, 151-160, 1979

Answer to Exercise 1

Report No. .... Date ....

An investigation into the effects of six primary fixatives on gelatin plugs

Materials and Methods

Six plugs were taken, using a cork bore, from 10% gelatin solidified in petri dishes and their dimensions were measured. One plug was placed in each of six test tubes. Each test tube was half filled with one of the following primary fixatives:

absolute alcohol	saturated mercuric chloride	glacial acetic acid
formaldehyde (10%)	potassium dichromate (1.5%)	saturated aqueous picric acid

The test tubes were left for 48 hours.

Results

The gelatin plugs initially measured 8 mm in diameter and 2 mm in depth.
Gelatin is a proteinaceous derivative of collagen.

Observations on gelatin plugs after 48 hours in different fixatives

FIXATIVE	CONDITION	COLOUR	HARDENING	SIZE (mm)
absolute alcohol	entire	white	hardened	5 x 2
saturated mercuric chloride	entire	white	hardened	7 x 2
glacial acetic acid	almost dissolved	clear	no hardening	2 x 0.5
formaldehyde 10%	entire	clear	hardened	10 x 4
potassium dichromate 1.5%	entire: adhering to bottom of tube	orange	hardened	6 x 1
saturated aq. picric acid	entire: adhering to bottom of tube	yellow	no/little hardening	2 x 0.5

Discussion

The different primary fixatives were found to have different effects on the gelatin plugs. Of particular importance are those effects related to shrinkage/swelling (alteration of plug size) and also to hardening of the plug.

Hardening of the plug was achieved by absolute alcohol, saturated mercuric chloride, formaldehyde and potassium dichromate. This is a necessary and desirable effect of a fixative, since hardening enables tissue to be handled more easily and it also safeguards tissue against the damaging effects of subsequent processing.

Alteration of plug size is obviously less desirable since the aim of a fixative is to preserve tissue in as 'life-like' a state as possible. Absolute alcohol, potassium dichromate and saturated aqueous picric acid were found to produce excessive shrinkage of the gelatin plug; saturated mercuric chloride caused slight shrinkage; formaldehyde caused slight swelling. In this context 10% formaldehyde would appear to be the best primary fixative of the six investigated. (Glacial acetic acid appeared to dissolve the gelatin plug and hence its swelling/shrinkage characteristics were difficult to ascertain.)

Answer to Exercise 3

A decent, though not definitive, version of the final table might look like the one shown below, which is arrived at by the following steps.

1   What is the purpose of the table? To record reaction velocities as a function of detergent type, so the layout begins thus
Detergent   Velocity of reaction

2   How many reactions? Two: E1, E2, hence
Detergent   Velocity of reaction
               E1   E2

3   What do we know about the distribution of assay systems used? E1 uses A, B; E2 uses C, D, E, so we get
Detergent   Velocity of reaction
               E1 assayed by   E2 assayed by
               A   B   C   D   E

4   What have we omitted? Quinone type and units, which gives the following completed table.

Detergent	Quinone	Velocity of reaction (U)				
		E1 assayed by		*E2 assayed by*		
		A	B	C	D	E
Triton X-100	Q-10	2000	400	1300	500	400
Octyl glucoside	Q-10	2200	-	-	-	-
Triton X-100	Q-2	2300	600	-	800	700
Triton X-165	Q-2	2200	1300	-	1100	1100
Emulphogen	Q-2	2100	300	-	200	200
Brij 35	Q-2	2100	2000	-	1100	1000
Brij 56	Q-2	2300	700	-	300	400
Brij 58	Q-2	2100	1000	-	600	600
Tween 20	Q-2	2400	1000	-	900	1000
Tween 80	Q-2	2300	1000	-	800	800

Exercise No 12

253 Ideas for Your Teaching

Instructions for the organiser: how to run a do-it-yourself activity using *253 Ideas for Your Teaching*
(Graham Gibbs & Trevor Habeshaw 3rd edn. 1992)

Timing
The exercise as designed can be completed comfortably by a group or groups of 12 participants in 2 hours. (Smaller groups can spend more time on the rounds or finish earlier. Larger groups can spend less time on the rounds or spend longer on the exercise overall.)

Group size
Minimum number of participants:	8
Ideal number of participants:	12
Maximum number of participants:	15

Large numbers of participants (there is no top limit) should be subdivided into groups of 8 - 15 members.

Accommodation
Ideally there should be a separate working area for each group of 8 - 15 participants, with enough space to set out a circle of chairs in the centre, and tables against the walls.
(If, through shortage of suitable accommodation, you are obliged to run the exercise for several groups in one room, it is advisable to keep the size of the groups small.)

Materials
Copies of *253 Ideas for Your Teaching* (see below).
All handouts for participants are provided in the pages which follow.

Before the event
1   Decide how you want to use the book, *253 Ideas for Your Teaching*. These are your options.

Option 1: every participant is given a copy of the book
In this case you will need to buy *one book for each participant*.

Option 2: every participant is given the same section of the book
In this case you will need to buy *one book only*. (You may want to choose this option if all participants are, for example, language teachers or science teachers.)
Select a section and make a photocopy of it for each participant.
(Copyright is waived for this option.)

Option 3: participants select a section of the book to work with
In this case you will need to buy *one book for each group of eight participants.*
Pull the books to pieces (physically) so that each book is in its ten separate sections.

(Copies of *253 Ideas for Your Teaching* are obtainable from Plymbridge Distributors Customer
Services at the contact address at the front of this book.)

2   Make a copy for each participant of the following materials:
   a   *Handout for participants*
   b   *Risk & Support Map*
   and single copies of the following materials:
   c   *Instructions for the announcer* (select the version for option 1, 2 or 3)
   d   *Instructions for the timekeeper* (select the version for option 1, 2 or 3)
   (If you have more than one group, you will need single copies of **c** and **d** for each group.)
   (Copyright is waived for these handouts.)

Immediately before the event
1   Set out chairs in a circle or circles.

2   On a side table set out
   a   *Instructions for the announcer*
   b   *Instructions for the timekeeper*

3   **Option 3:** lay out the ten sections of *253 Ideas for Your Teaching* on tables for each group of
   eight participants.

At the event
1   Ensure that every participant picks up the ***Risk and Support Map*** and reads the ***handout for
   participants*** on entering the room.

2   **Option 1:** give every participant a copy of *253 Ideas for Your Teaching*.
   Option 2: give every participant a copy of the section you have selected.

3   Join the exercise as an *equal* participant.

Handout for participants

Glance quickly through these notes.

1 This is a 'do-it-yourself' workshop. All the necessary instructions are provided, although to start the workshop requires a bit of organisation for which your cooperation is required.

2 The person whose name comes *first* alphabetically should take the *Instructions for the announcer*.

3 The person whose name comes *last* alphabetically should take the *Instructions for the timekeeper*.

4 The announcer and timekeeper will need a couple of minutes to glance through their instructions, then the announcer will start the workshop.

5 Everyone, including the announcer and the timekeeper, takes part in the exercise as an equal participant.

6 Enjoy yourself.

RISK AND SUPPORT MAP

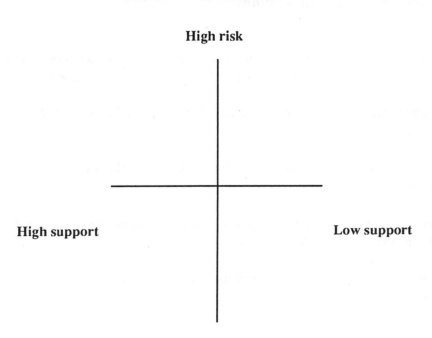

High risk

High support   **Low support**

Low risk

1   Look through the items from the book *253 Ideas For Your Teaching* which you have been given. Think of things you could do which involve you in different amounts of risk, and also of things for which you would require different amounts of support, and choose four items, **one** item to fit into each quadrant of the map. Write them in. (15 minutes)

2   Discuss with your partner the reasons which led you to place each item in its particular quadrant, and what support you would need (if any) in order to be able to implement the ideas in your classes. (5 minutes each)

Instructions for the announcer (option 1)

Glance quickly through these instructions.

1   Get everyone's attention and read out the following message:

> I am the announcer and I have to announce things to you. The authors of the book we will be using have sent this message to you:
>
> > *In this session you will be thinking about new teaching methods which you could introduce into your own courses. There are so many ideas on offer here that we are sure you will find methods that are new to you and which seem attractive and potentially useful.*
> >
> > *We believe that 'experts' are not always useful during such discussions and we are confident that you can have a productive and enjoyable session by yourselves.*
>
> There are no other instructions than these I am reading now. If you are confused, don't ask ME; use your common sense.
>
> The first thing to do is to introduce ourselves. We'll do a 'round', starting with the person on my right and moving anticlockwise. We've got a few minutes to complete the round and for each of us to say who we are and what we teach. O.K., let's start with the person on my right.

2   At the end of the round please read the following:

> You have been given copies of *253 Ideas for Your Teaching* and copies of the *Risk and Support Map*. Has everyone got these?

If everyone has, then say:

> We are asked to imagine that we are about to try something new in teaching one of our courses. We are to look through the book and think about changes in teaching methods which we'd like to introduce. We are to try to identify one change which would fit into each quadrant of the *Risk and Support Map*. We'll have 8 minutes to look at the book and 7 minutes to write something in each quadrant, making 15 minutes in total. After this the timekeeper will tell us to move on to the next stage of the activity. We will be asked to get together with one other person and tell them a little about the course we've been thinking of, and to talk about the ideas that we'd like to introduce, about the educational benefits which these ideas would bring and any other reasons why it would be a good thing to introduce these changes. We are also to talk about the risk these changes might

entail and what support we might need to carry them through successfully. **We'll have five minutes each to talk through our maps. We will take turns, each acting as speaker and listener. The timekeeper will tell us when each set of five minutes is up.**

O.K., you have the books. The instructions for the task are on your *Risk and Support Map*. You have fifteen minutes, starting now.

N.B. Remember to participate yourself.

3   After the timekeeper has announced *You've now had 15 minutes. It's time to get into pairs now,* and everyone has paired up, please read the following:

I have an announcement. Just to remind you what you should be doing, you have 5 minutes each to talk with your partner about your *Risk and Support Map*. The instructions are on the map. The timekeeper will tell us when each five minutes is up.

4   After each person has spoken and the timekeeper has announced that the 10 minutes is up, say:

I have an announcement. We have all now had a chance to talk about teaching methods we'd like to introduce on one of our own courses. Let's go round and see what people want to try out, and why, and what they have to say about 'risk' and 'support'.

Starting with the pair opposite me, and moving round in a clockwise direction, each person in turn has five minutes to tell the group about an idea which they'd like to introduce. Other members of the group can ask questions and make comments before we move on to the next person.

The timekeeper will tell us when five minutes are up for each person.

5   When everyone has had their turn read out this announcement:

Thank you for taking part in this exercise. That is the end of the session.

Instructions for the announcer (option 2)

Glance quickly through these instructions.

1   Get everyone's attention and read out the following message:

I am the announcer and I have to announce things to you. The authors of the book we will be using have sent this message to you:
> *In this session you will be thinking about new teaching methods which you could introduce into your own courses.*
> *We believe that 'experts' are not always useful during such discussions and we are confident that you can have a productive and enjoyable session by yourselves.*

There are no other instructions than these I am reading now. If you are confused, don't ask ME; use your common sense.

The first thing to do is to introduce ourselves. We'll do a 'round', starting with the person on my right and moving anticlockwise. We've got a few minutes to complete the round and for each of us to say who we are and what we teach. O.K., let's start with the person on my right.

2   At the end of the round please read the following:

You have been given copies of a section of the book, *253 Ideas for Your Teaching*, and copies of the *Risk and Support Map*. Has everyone got these?

If everyone has, then say:

We are asked to imagine that we are about to try something new in teaching one of our courses. We are to look through the material and think about changes in teaching methods which we'd like to introduce. We are to try to identify one change which would fit into each quadrant of the *Risk and Support Map*. We'll have 8 minutes to look at the material and 7 minutes to write something in each quadrant, making 15 minutes in total. After this the timekeeper will tell us to move on to the next stage of the activity. We will be asked to get together with one other person and tell them a little about the course we've been thinking of, and to talk about the ideas that we'd like to introduce, about the educational benefits which these ideas would bring and any other reasons why it would be a good thing to introduce these changes. We are also to talk about the risk these changes might entail and

what support we might need to carry them through successfully. We'll have five minutes each to talk through our maps. We will take turns, each acting as speaker and listener.

The timekeeper will tell us when each set of five minutes is up.

O.K., you have the material. The instructions for the task are on your *Risk and Support Map*. You have fifteen minutes, starting now.

N.B. Remember to participate yourself.

3   After the timekeeper has announced *You've now had 15 minutes. It's time to get into pairs now,* and everyone has paired up, please read the following:

I have an announcement. Just to remind you what you should be doing, you have 5 minutes each to talk with your partner about your *Risk and Support Map*. The instructions are on the map. The timekeeper will tell us when each five minutes is up.

4   After each person has spoken and the timekeeper has announced that the 10 minutes is up, say:

I have an announcement. We have all now had a chance to talk about teaching methods we'd like to introduce on one of our own courses. Let's go round and see what people want to try out, and why, and what they have to say about 'risk' and 'support'.

Starting with the pair opposite me, and moving round in a clockwise direction, each person in turn has five minutes to tell the group about an idea which they'd like to introduce. Other members of the group can ask questions and make comments before we move on to the next person.

The timekeeper will tell us when five minutes are up for each person.

5   When everyone has had their turn read out this announcement:

Thank you for taking part in this exercise. That is the end of the session.

Instructions for the announcer (option 3)

Glance quickly through these instructions.

1   Get everyone's attention and read out the following message:

> I am the announcer and I have to announce things to you. The authors of the book we will be using have sent this message to you:
>
> > *In this session you will be thinking about new teaching methods which you could introduce into your own courses.*
> >
> > *We believe that 'experts' are not always useful during such discussions and we are confident that you can have a productive and enjoyable session by yourselves.*
>
> There are no other instructions than these I am reading now. If you are confused, don't ask ME; use your common sense.
>
> The first thing to do is to introduce ourselves. We'll do a 'round', starting with the person on my right and moving anticlockwise. We've got a few minutes to complete the round and for each of us to say who we are and what we teach. O.K., let's start with the person on my right.

2   At the end of the round please read the following:

> On the tables are the ten sections of *253 Ideas for Your Teaching*. Please go and choose one to work with and bring it back to the circle of chairs.

3   When everyone has chosen a section, read out the following:

> We are asked to imagine that we are about to try something new in teaching one of our courses. We are to look through the material and think about changes in teaching methods which we'd like to introduce. We are to try to identify one change which would fit into each quadrant of the *Risk and Support Map*. (You've got a copy of the *Risk and Support Map* on a separate sheet). We'll have 8 minutes to look at the material and 7 minutes to write something in each quadrant, making 15 minutes in total. After this the timekeeper will tell us to move on to the next stage of the activity. We will be asked to get together with one other person and tell them a little about the course we've been thinking of, and to talk about the ideas that we'd like to introduce, about the educational benefits which these ideas would bring and any other reasons why it would be a good thing to introduce these changes. We are also to talk about the risk these changes might entail and what support we might need

to carry them through successfully. We'll have five minutes each to talk through our maps
We will take turns, each acting as speaker and listener. The timekeeper will tell us when
each set of five minutes is up.

O.K., you have the material. The instructions for the task are on your *Risk and Support Map*
You have fifteen minutes, starting now.

N.B. Remember to participate yourself.

4   After the timekeeper has announced *You've now had 15 minutes. It's time to get into pairs now*
    and everyone has paired up, please read the following:

    I have an announcement. Just to remind you what you should be doing, you have **5 minute**
    each to talk with your partner about your *Risk and Support Map*. The instructions are on
    the map. The timekeeper will tell us when each five minutes is up.

5   After each person has spoken and the timekeeper has announced that the 10 minutes is up, say

    I have an announcement. We have all now had a chance to talk about teaching method
    we'd like to introduce on one of our own courses. Let's go round and see what people wan
    to try out, and why, and what they have to say about 'risk' and 'support'.

    Starting with the pair opposite me, and moving round in a clockwise direction, each person
    in turn has five minutes to tell the group about an idea which they'd like to introduce. Othe
    members of the group can ask questions and make comments before we move on to the nex
    person.

    The timekeeper will tell us when five minutes are up for each person.

6   When everyone has had their turn read out this announcement:

    Thank you for taking part in this exercise. That is the end of the session.

Instructions for the timekeeper (option 1)

Glance quickly through these instructions.

It is your job to inform others when the time allocated for a task has elapsed. Otherwise you should participate like everyone else.

1   People have 8 minutes to look at the book and 7 minutes to work on the *Risk and Support Map*. Let them know when the time has elapsed by saying:

You have had your 8 minutes' reading time. Now you have 7 minutes to write on your *Risk and Support Map*.

and

You've now had 15 minutes. It's time to get into pairs now.

2   When people are sitting in pairs taking turns to talk through their *Risk and Support Map*, they should have five minutes each. At the end of the first five minutes, please say:

You have had five minutes now. Please swop round. Now the other person has five minutes.

3   When the second period of five minutes is up, say:

You have had ten minutes now. Please come back into the circle.

4   When people are in the circle and taking turns to describe what they've decided to try out in their courses, let them know how much time they have had by saying:

We've now spent 5 minutes on this idea. It is time to move on to the next person.

Instructions for the timekeeper (option 2)

Glance quickly through these instructions.

It is your job to inform others when the time allocated for a task has elapsed. Otherwise you should participate like everyone else.

1   People have 8 minutes to look at the section of the book and 7 minutes to work on the *Risk and Support Map*. Let them know when the time has elapsed by saying:

You have had your 8 minutes' reading time. Now you have 7 minutes to write on your *Risk and Support Map*.

and

You've now had 15 minutes. It's time to get into pairs now.

2   When people are sitting in pairs taking turns to talk through their *Risk and Support Map*, they should have five minutes each. At the end of the first five minutes, please say:

You have had five minutes now. Please swop round. Now the other person has five minutes.

When the second period of five minutes is up, say:

You have had ten minutes now. Please come back into the circle.

3   When people are in the circle and taking turns to describe what they've decided to try out in their courses, let them know how much time they have had by saying:

We've now spent 5 minutes on this idea. It is time to move on to the next person.

nstructions for the timekeeper (option 3)

ʒlance quickly through these instructions.

t is your job to inform others when the time allocated for a task has elapsed. Otherwise you should articipate like everyone else.

People have 8 minutes to look at their chosen section of the book and 7 minutes to work on the *Risk and Support Map*. Let them know when the time has elapsed by saying:

You have had your 8 minutes' reading time. Now you have 7 minutes to write on your *Risk and Support Map*.

and

You've now had 15 minutes. It's time to get into pairs now.

When people are sitting in pairs taking turns to talk through their *Risk and Support Map*, they should have five minutes each. At the end of the first five minutes, please say:

You have had five minutes now. Please swop round. Now the other person has five minutes.

When the second period of five minutes is up, say:

You have had ten minutes now. Please come back into the circle.

When people are in the circle and taking turns to describe what they've decided to try out in their courses, let them know how much time they have had by saying:

We've now spent 5 minutes on this idea. It is time to move on to the next person.